Discover London

by Juliana O'Neill

© 2017 by Juliana O'Neill
ISBN: 978-1-53240-2630
eISBN: 978-1-53240-2647
Images licensed from Fotolia.com
All rights reserved.
No portion of this book may be reproduced
without express permission of the publisher.
First Edition
Published in the United States by
Xist Publishing
www.xistpublishing.com
PO Box 61593 Irvine, CA 92602

London is a very old city. There have been people in the London area for more than 3,000 years.

The city was formed by the Roman Empire. The Romans invaded Briton in 43 AD and started the city of Londonium shortly after. It was a very small city.

Today, London is a very big city. London is the capital of England and also the United Kingdom.

The United Kingdom is made up of England, Scotland, Wales and Northern Ireland.

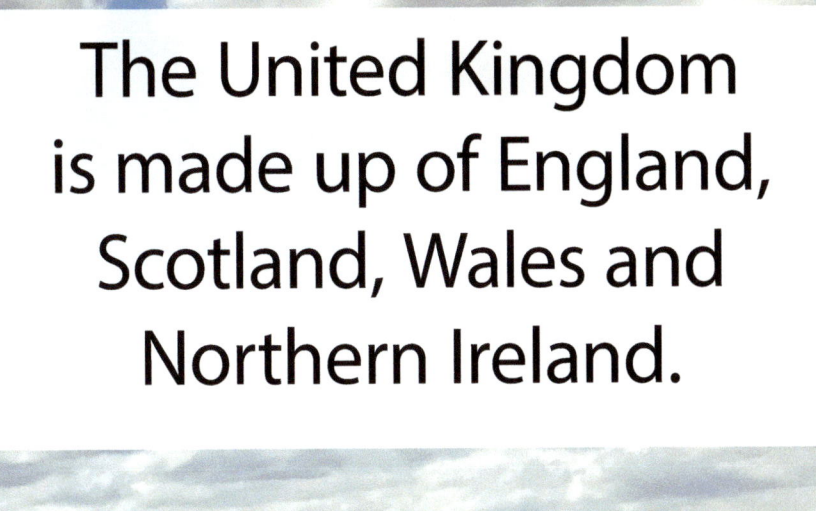

As a capital city, London is home the offices of government. The Palace of Westminster is where the Houses of Parliament meet.

Big Ben is the name of the bell inside this famous bell tower. It was once named the Clock Tower but was renamed the Elizabeth Tower in 2012. However, most people still call the tower Big Ben.

The main river of London is called the Thames (Pronounced Tems). The Thames was once used for moving people and goods into and around the city.

The London Eye is a new addition to the old city of London. It is a giant Ferris wheel that goes 443 feet (135 meters) into the sky. It gives people a great view of the city below.

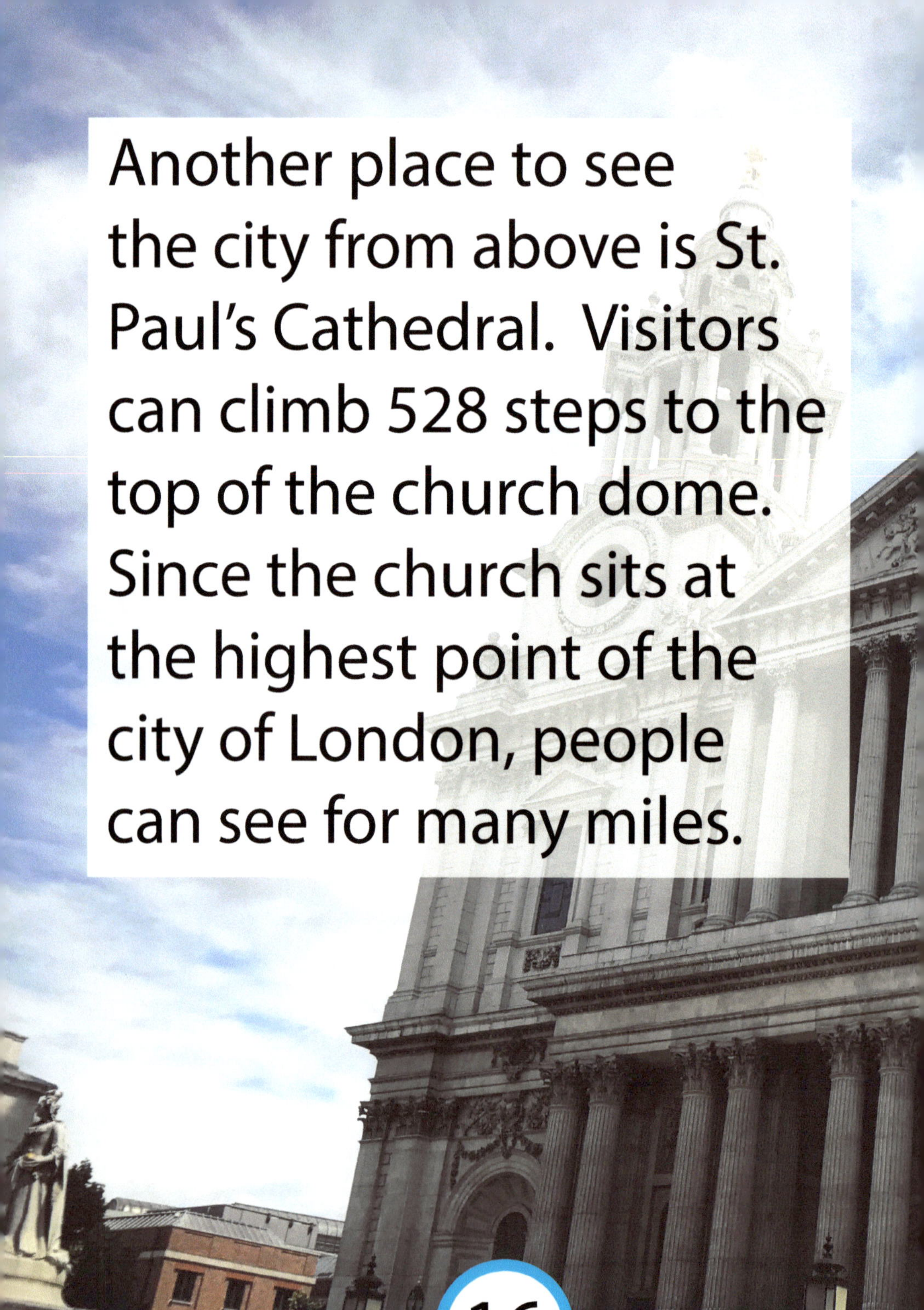

Another place to see the city from above is St. Paul's Cathedral. Visitors can climb 528 steps to the top of the church dome. Since the church sits at the highest point of the city of London, people can see for many miles.

Shakespeare's Globe Theater is a newer version of a very old theater. The theater was first built in 1599 and was the place where many famous plays were performed. The first Globe Theater burned down in 1613 and the second was torn down in 1644.

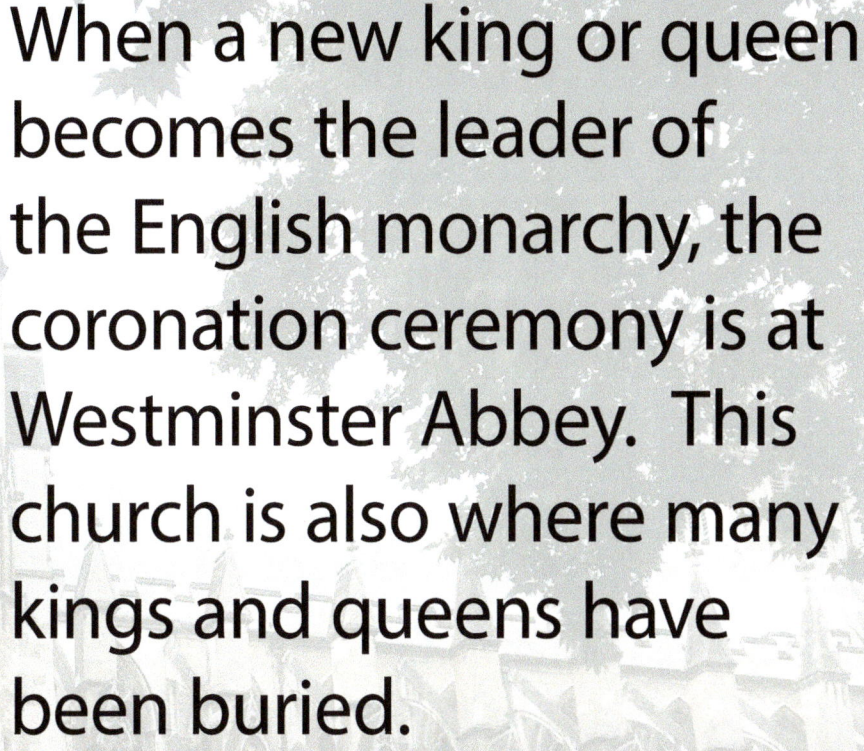

When a new king or queen becomes the leader of the English monarchy, the coronation ceremony is at Westminster Abbey. This church is also where many kings and queens have been buried.

This historic castle has been a palace, a prison and is now a museum. The Tower of London was once where political prisoners were held and tortured. Now it is home to the crown jewels, suits of armor and many other royal treasures.

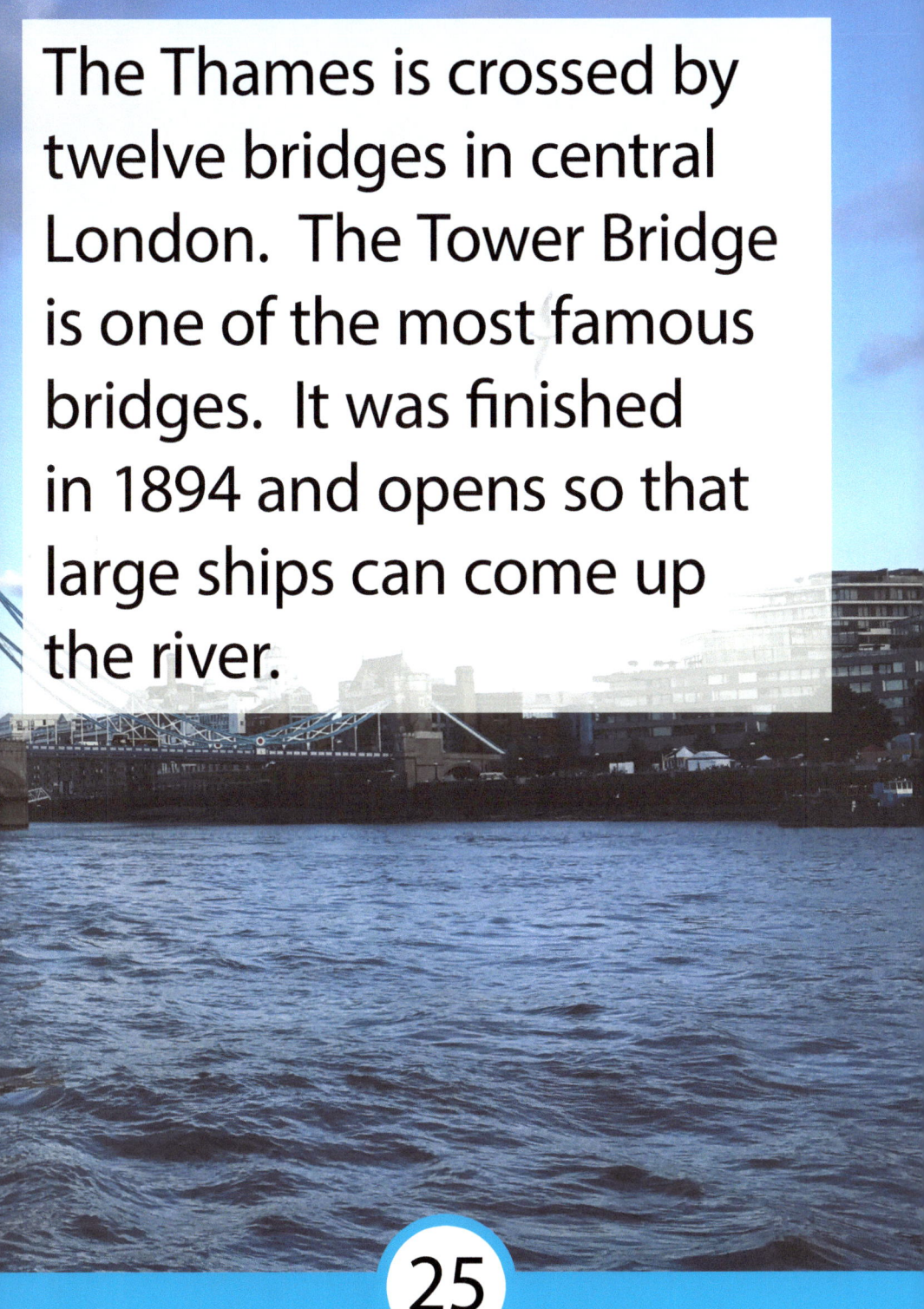

The Thames is crossed by twelve bridges in central London. The Tower Bridge is one of the most famous bridges. It was finished in 1894 and opens so that large ships can come up the river.

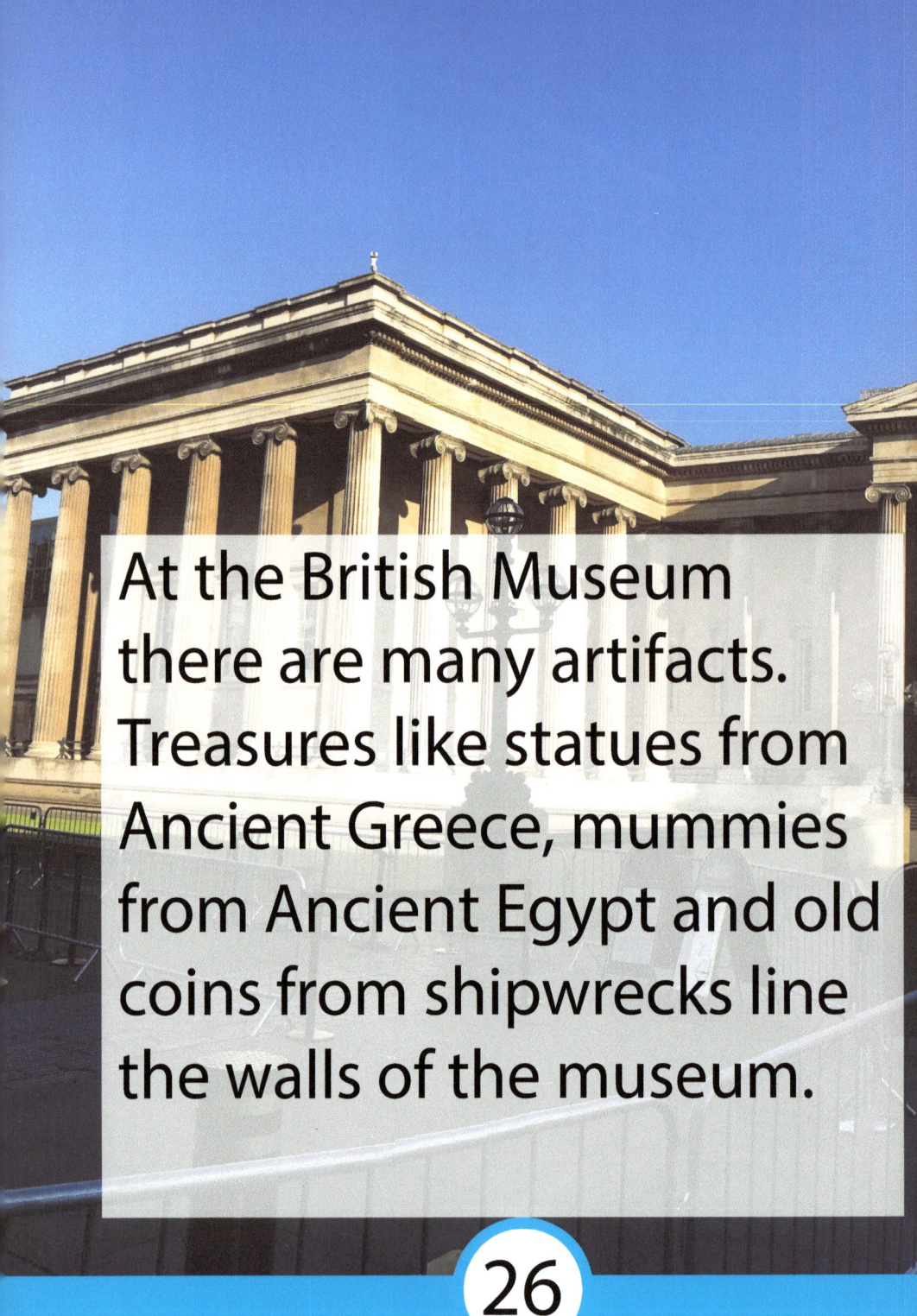

At the British Museum there are many artifacts. Treasures like statues from Ancient Greece, mummies from Ancient Egypt and old coins from shipwrecks line the walls of the museum.

Buckingham Palace is the London home of the royal family. It is a symbol of the monarchy, an art gallery and a tourist attraction.

www.ingramcontent.com/pod-product-compliance
Lightning Source LLC
LaVergne TN
LVHW010021070426
835507LV00001B/31